# Birds
## North of America
VOLUME 1

designed by
Brian McMillan
Lucinda Doran

Photography
Brian McMillan

Layout
Gerald Loewen

Published in Canada
by

**Walrus Publications**

Copyright © 1994 by

**Walrus Publications**

All rights reserved

No part of this book may be reproduced for any reason except for personal use in constructing a project.
Any form of commercial reproduction is forbidden except by written permission from the publisher.

ISBN 0 921520-02-6

Printed in Canada

# GLASS CLASS HINTS

Birds and stained glass just seem to be a natural pair. The wonderful mixes of color in opalescent glass lend themselves beautifully to be used as feathers in birds. However, eyes and feet can often present problems. The following are some of the ways that we have tried to solve these details. They may work for you - or maybe you will see a better solution. Either way I hope that you enjoy building these projects.

## Eyes

The simplest way to deal with eyes is to paint them on to the glass. We have found that the best is sign painter's paints which can usually be purchased at hobby stores. If you can't find this type then any acrylic or model paint will do. Often you are painting a black eye on dark glass. If this is the case, sometimes it is best to use white paint first and then paint a black pupil - making sure to leave a bit of the white showing.

In most cases it is preferable to have an eye cut out of glass. Sometimes, as in the case of the Pintail and Loon, the pieces of glass become so small that if you foil them they disappear. We have had good luck just dropping the unfoiled piece of glass into its proper opening and then soldering as usual. The foil of the adjoining pieces will allow the solder to hold the eye in place.

## Legs and Feet

Legs and feet present another challenge. Because most birds are done life size the legs and feet are too thin to cut out of glass. Often wire works well - as with the Goldfinch and Cardinal. 14 or 16 gauge wire (copper, brass or pretinned copper) works best as it is easy to bend and will take solder and patina well. Also you can twist two or three pieces of wire together if you need a thicker leg.

Another possibility is to use a copper foil overlay such as we did with the Red-Winged Blackbird. In this case you cut a piece of sheet copper (it is available in 12 inch x 12 inch squares) to the proper shape. Flux it and bead solder it. It is usually best to do this on a piece of plywood as the heat will often crack the glass. Once it has cooled it is just a matter of attaching the overlay whenever it touches a solder seam. Or sometimes you can just leave a space between the pieces of glass and fill it with solder. This worked well on the Robin. Use 50/50 solder to fill the void. Let it cool and then bead (or round) the seams using 60/40 solder.

## Edge Treatments

When constructing the duck decoys and bird mobiles you will often find that some pieces of glass will be too flexible and will require extra support. A good example would be the two top tail feathers of the Pintail. It is important to solder a 20 gauge wire either around the entire project for extra support or at least 2 inches past the problem pieces. When soldering on wire it is best to tack solder it on to the copper foil on the edge of the project every 1/2 inch.

Since wire conducts heat very well it is a good idea to wear rubber gloves when soldering it. Be careful to bend it accurately around all deep curves on your project. Once it has been tacked on all the way around, bead the edge as you would any copper foil project.

On the Woodpecker panel, instead of wire we used ball chain (the same stuff that is used as pull chain on lamps). It is attached in the same manner as the wire. Also any solderable fine chain works well.

## Using Brass Rings for Borders

The Owl and Robin panels feature brass rings for their borders. These are commonly used for macramé and can be purchased at craft stores. Try to get one that is brass-plated so that it will solder well. If it isn't brass-plated and won't solder well you can wrap the areas of the ring which you wish to solder with copper foil and then solder as usual. On the Owl panel we cut the ring so that it doesn't go behind the moon - however, the tail feathers just sit in front of the ring.

## Wooden Bases for Duck Decoys

The duck decoys look great displayed standing in a wooden base. These should be available at your local stained glass shop or if you know a wood worker you can have them made to your own specifications. The ones we use are 7 inches wide, 4 inches deep and 3/4 of an inch thick with a slot cut into them which is 3/16 of an inch wide and 3/8 of an inch deep. It you find that your duck decoy wobbles in the base, you can glue it into the slot using clear silicone sealer. Make sure that you have it propped up at a suitable angle because once the silicone sets you will not be able to adjust it.

These duck decoys can also be hung in a window by simply soldering rings into two appropriate solder seams and then using fish line to suspend the piece from a suction cup or cup hook in the window frame. If the duck doesn't hang level you can often solve this problem by using two suction cups (or cup hooks) and either put the suction cup hook directly into the rings on the duck or tie the fish line onto the hooks of the cups as needed to keep it level.

IT IS VERY IMPORTANT TO TEST SUCTION CUPS FREQUENTLY AND CHANGE FISH LINE AT LEAST ONCE A YEAR AS IT DECOMPOSES IN SUNLIGHT.

## Glass Selection

I would highly recommend spending some time at your local library looking at good quality photographs of the birds you wish to craft in stained glass. This will be time well spent when you arrive at your local stained glass store to choose glass. Some tips on glass selection are:

1. Generally it is best to use glass that is a shade brighter color than the actual bird.

2. Hand-rolled glass has more variation within the sheet which allows you to pick and choose parts of the glass for different effects. As an example, you can often find a piece of grey opal that is white in some spots with medium grey and dark grey patches. Using this glass effectively can add a look of realism to your work.

3. Opalescent glass is your best choice for birds but sometimes the color you need will only be available in cathedral or antique. This is often fine- especially for highlights.

Speaking of glass - as you are probably aware, to cut opalescent glass you must make a pattern, trace around it with a permanent pen and then cut along the inside of the pen line. Instead of cutting the pattern out of paper, use clear window glass. It's inexpensive, easy to cut and grind for a perfect fit and very durable. Just put the glass templates into an envelope with the name of the project on the front and it will be ready for future use.

# SPECIFICATIONS
# BIRD PANELS

## Blue Jay

Dimensions:
16 1/4 inches wide by 10 1/2 inches high

### MATERIALS

**Blue Jay** - White, blue, grey and black Opals
**Branch** - Brown Cathedral - 1/3 sq. ft.
**Moon** - Amber Craquelle or Cathedral
**Background** - Dark blue Cathedral

One length of 1/4 inch U zinc

### HINTS

The beak is an overlay of black glass. Clean and patina the main panel, solder and patina the beak and then solder it to the main panel. Carefully clean and patina the fresh solder.

## Screech Owl

Dimensions: 12 inch circle

### MATERIALS

**Owl** - Reddish brown Cathedrals and Opals
**Eyes** - Amber Cathedral
**Moon** - Blue Cathedral
**Branch** - Brown

One 12 inch brass ring
(see Glass Class Hints for soldering tips).

## Robin

Dimensions: 9 inch circle

### MATERIALS

**Robin** - Grey, white and orange Opal
**Worm** - Brown Opal
**Beak** - Amber
**Ground** - Green and amber Opal

One 9 inch brass ring (see Glass Class Hints for soldering tips.

## Loon

Dimensions: 20 inches wide by 12 inches high

### MATERIALS

**Loon** - Black and white Opal and black and clear Baroque
**Bill** - Dark grey Cathedral
**Eye** - Red Cathedral
**Trees** - Green Cathedral - 1/2 sq. ft.
**Beach** - Beige (honey) Opal - 1/3 sq. ft.
**Water** - Medium blue Cathedral - 1/2 sq. ft.
- Blue/green ripple Cathedral - 2/3 sq. ft.
**Cloud** - White Iridescent
**Bottom glass border** - Grey Cathedral
**Sky** - Light blue Cathedral - 1 sq. ft.
One length U lead for border

### HINTS

Try using one of the duck decoy patterns with this background instead of the loon to create your own design.

Red-Winged Blackbird

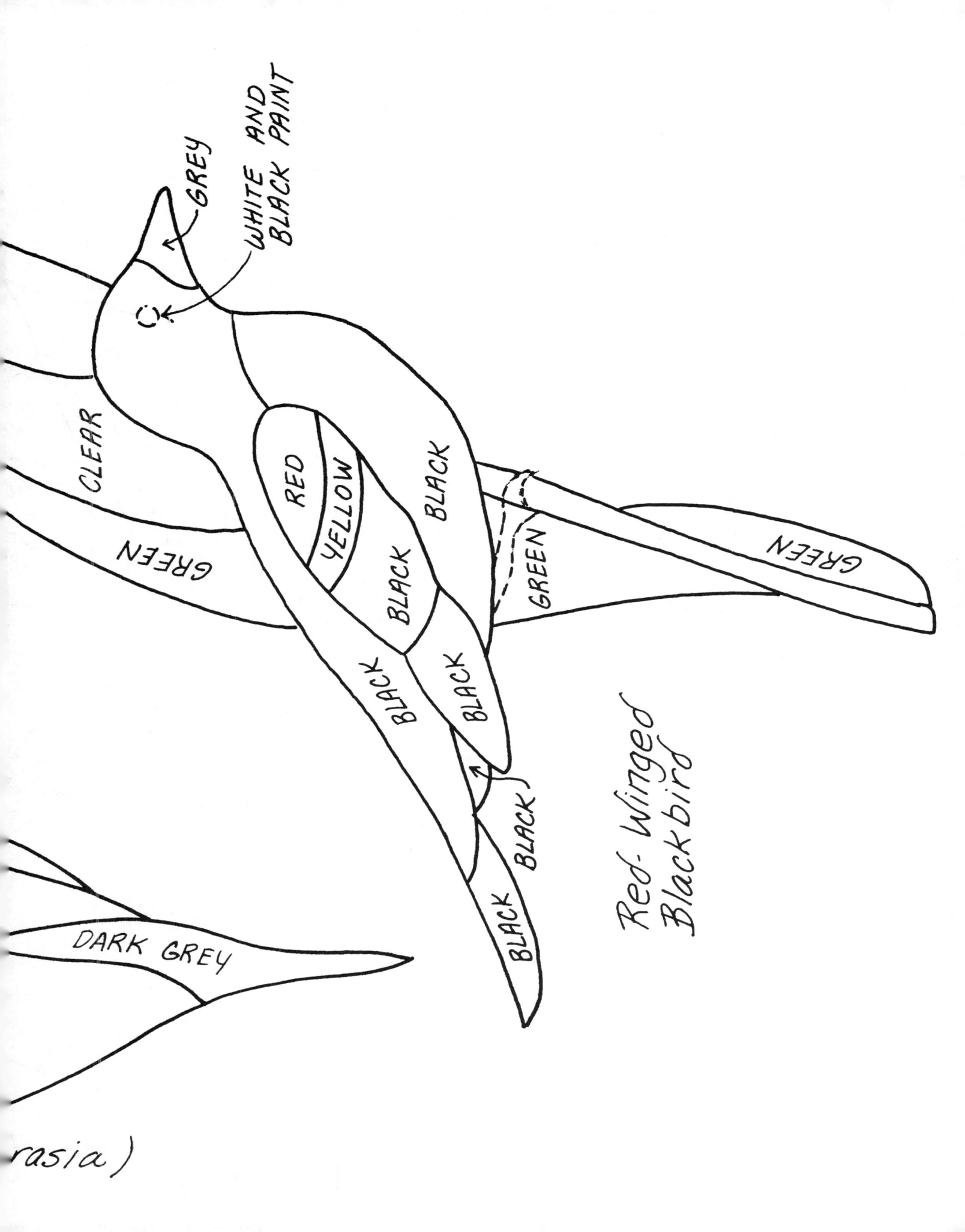

(rasia)

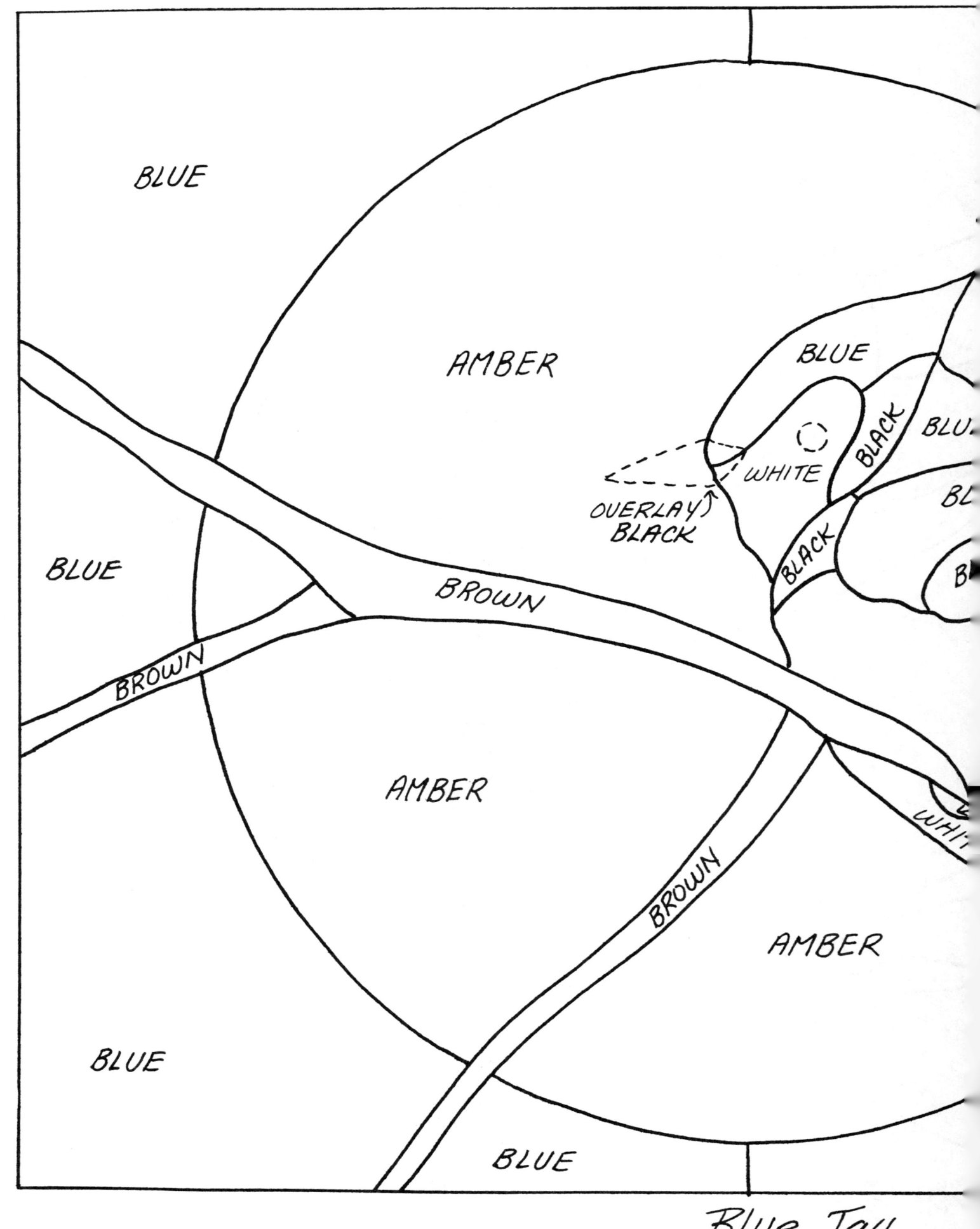

Blue Jay

Goldfinch

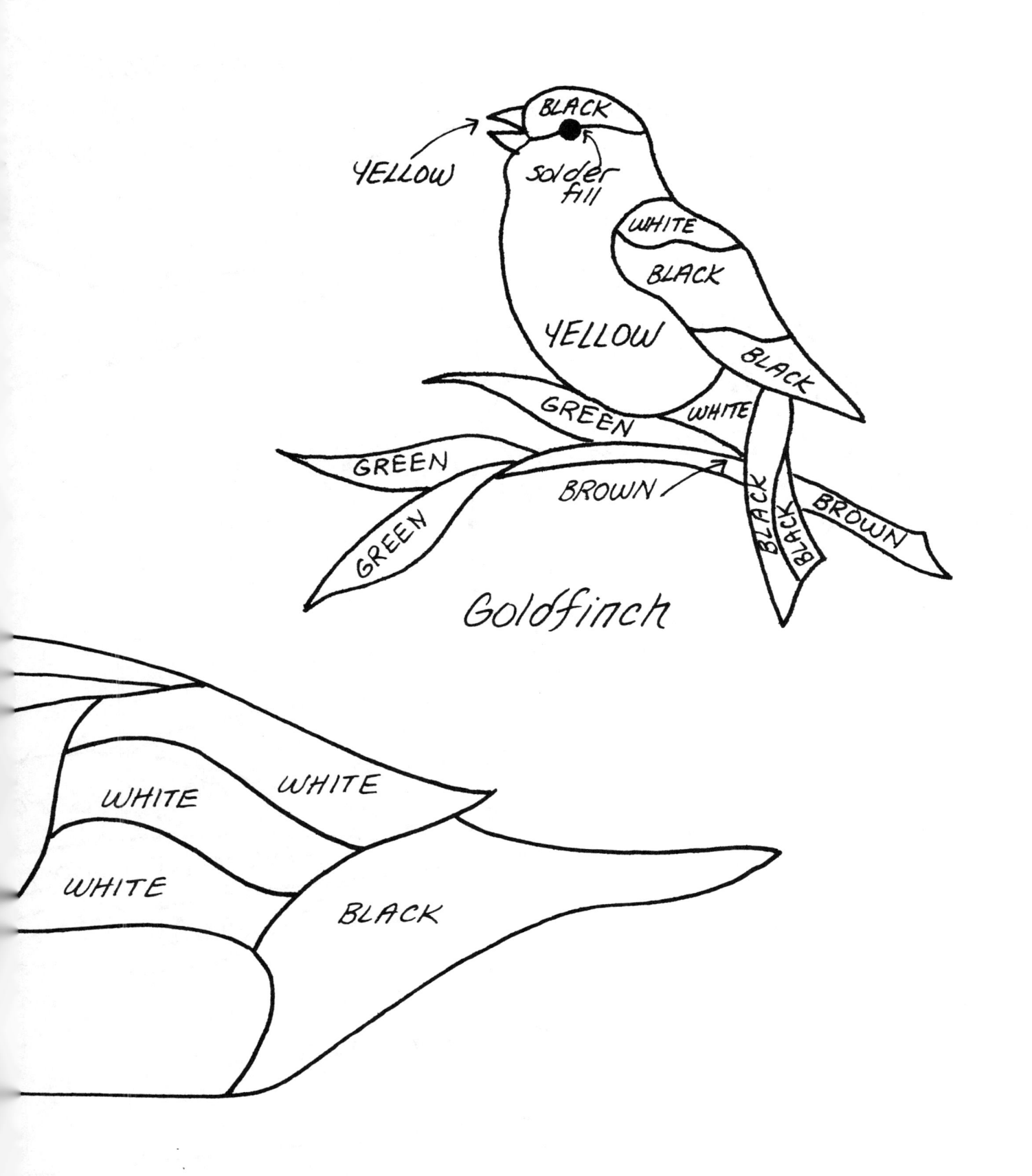

Pintail

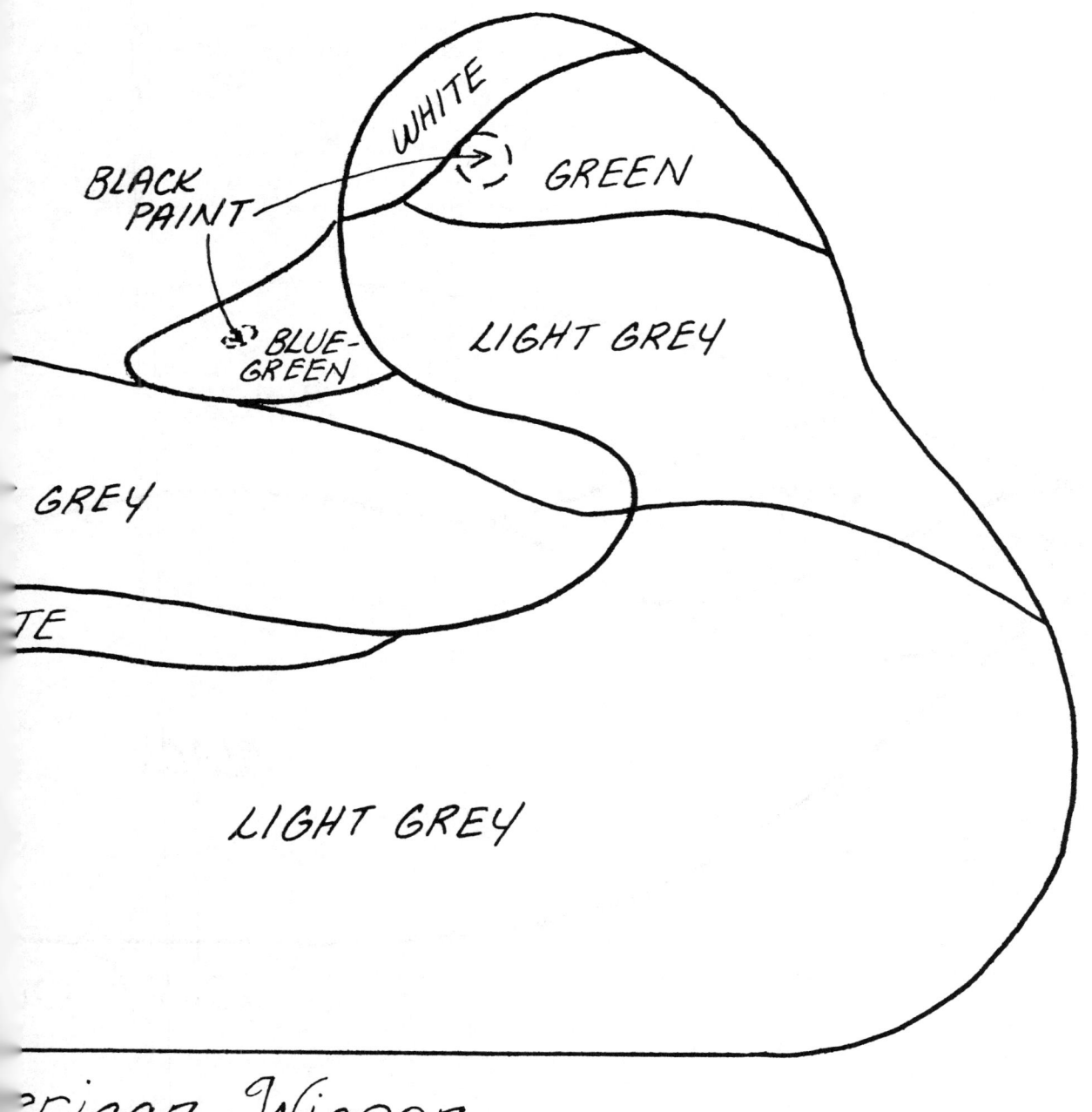

WHITE
BLACK PAINT
GREEN
BLUE-GREEN
LIGHT GREY
GREY
TE
LIGHT GREY

*rican Wigeon*

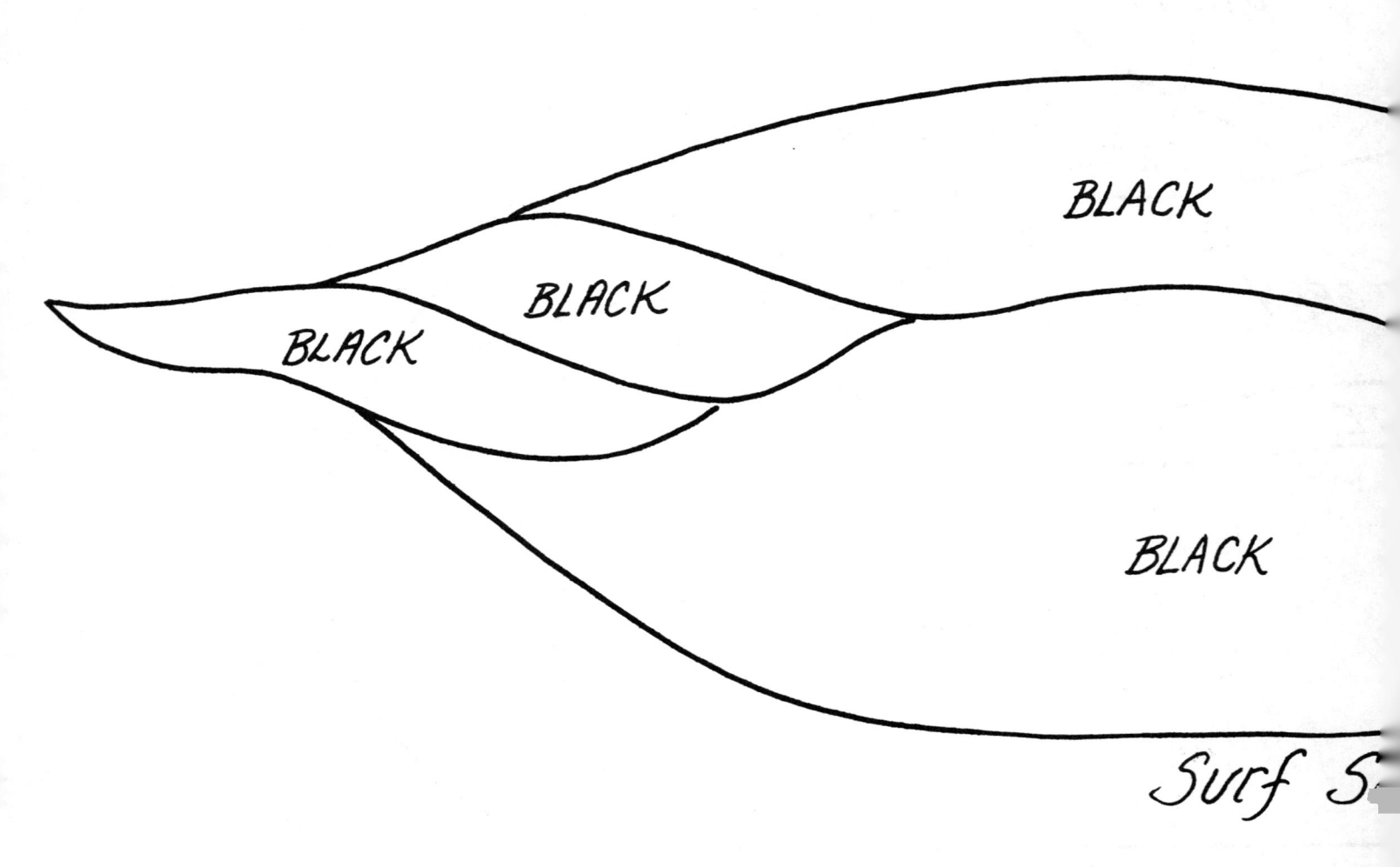

BLACK

BLACK

BLACK

BLACK

Surf S

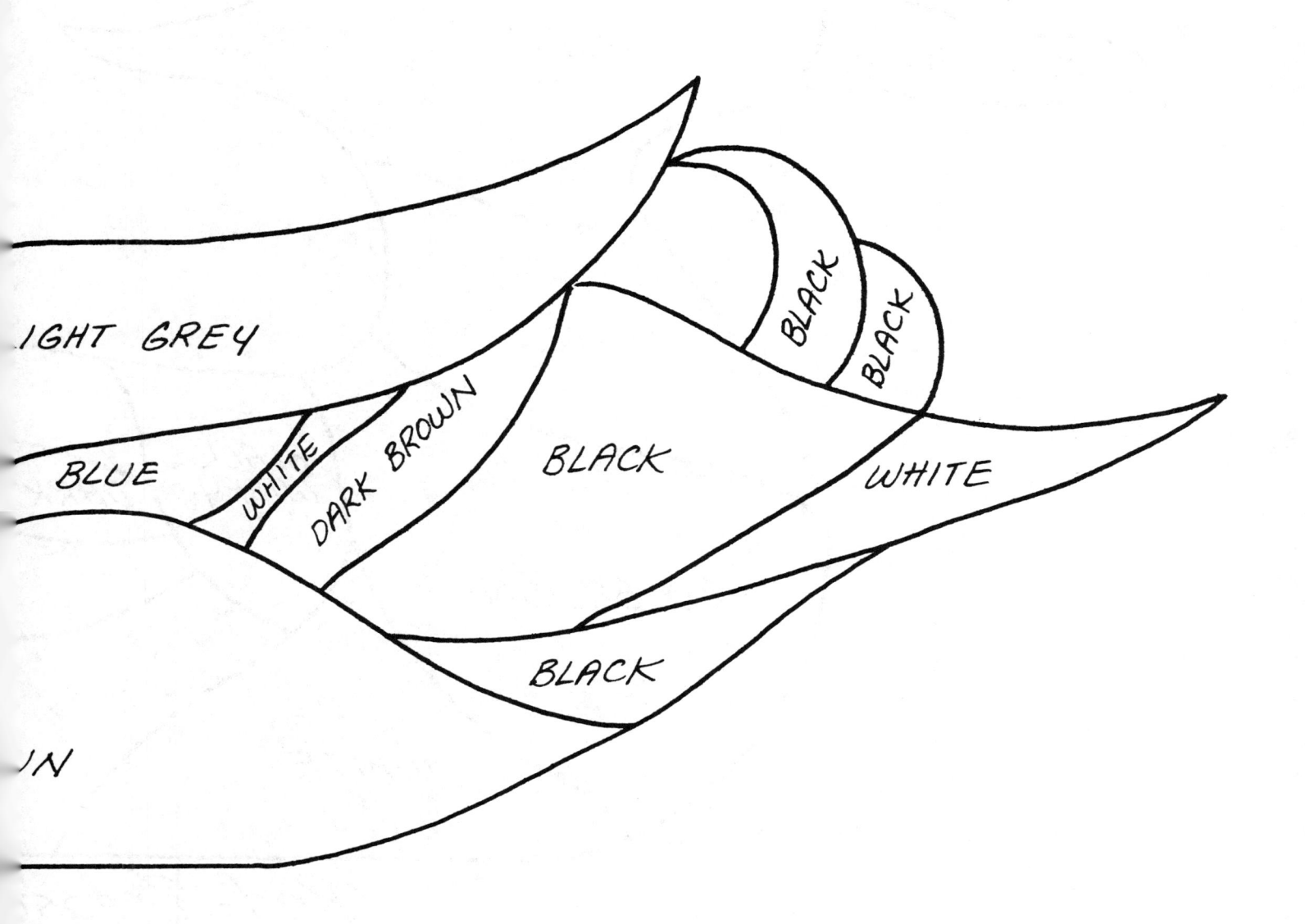

LIGHT GREY

BLUE  WHITE  DARK BROWN  BLACK  WHITE

BLACK  BLACK

BLACK

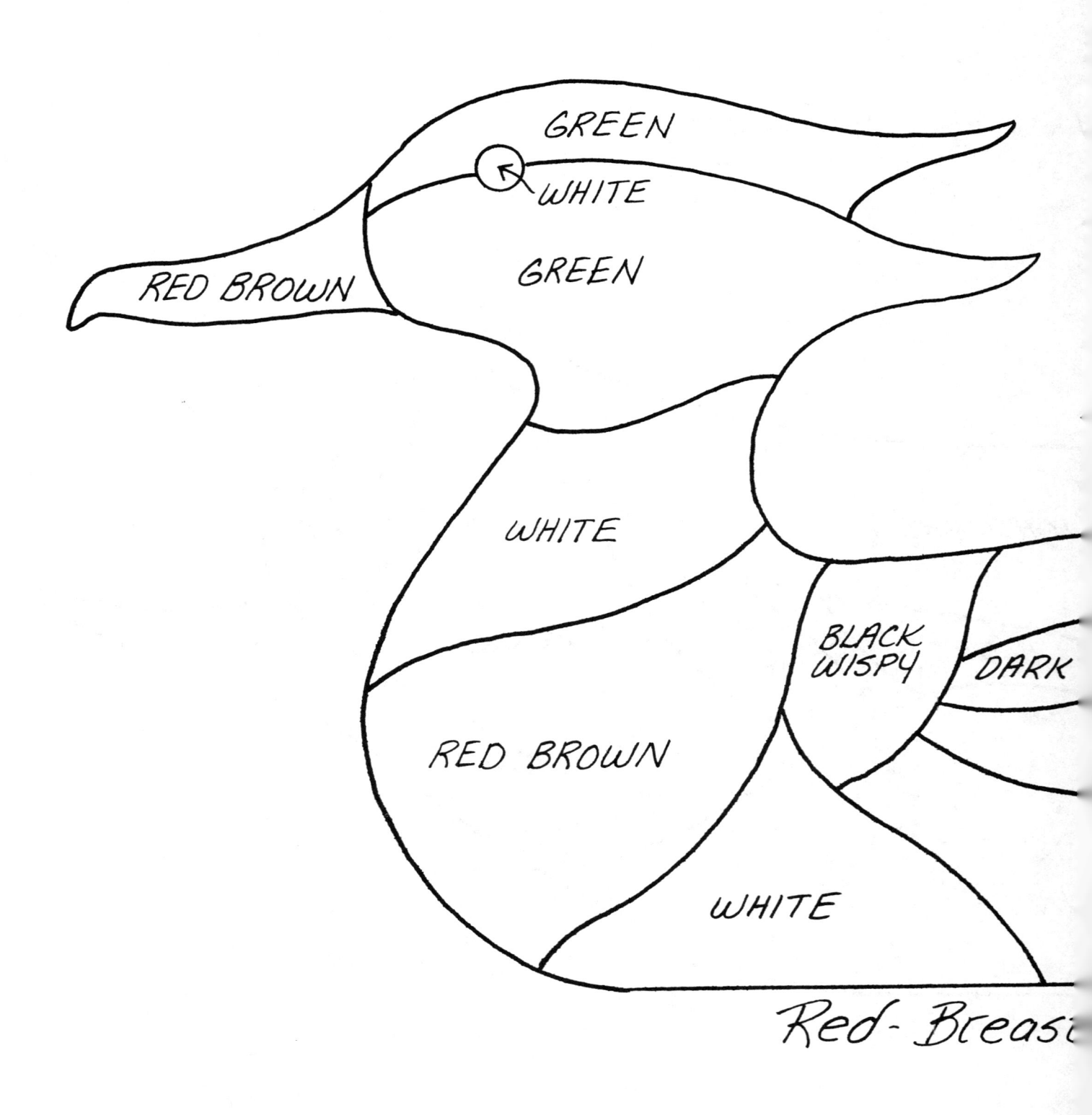

GREEN

WHITE

RED BROWN

GREEN

WHITE

BLACK WISPY

DARK

RED BROWN

WHITE

Red-Breas

—STREAMER

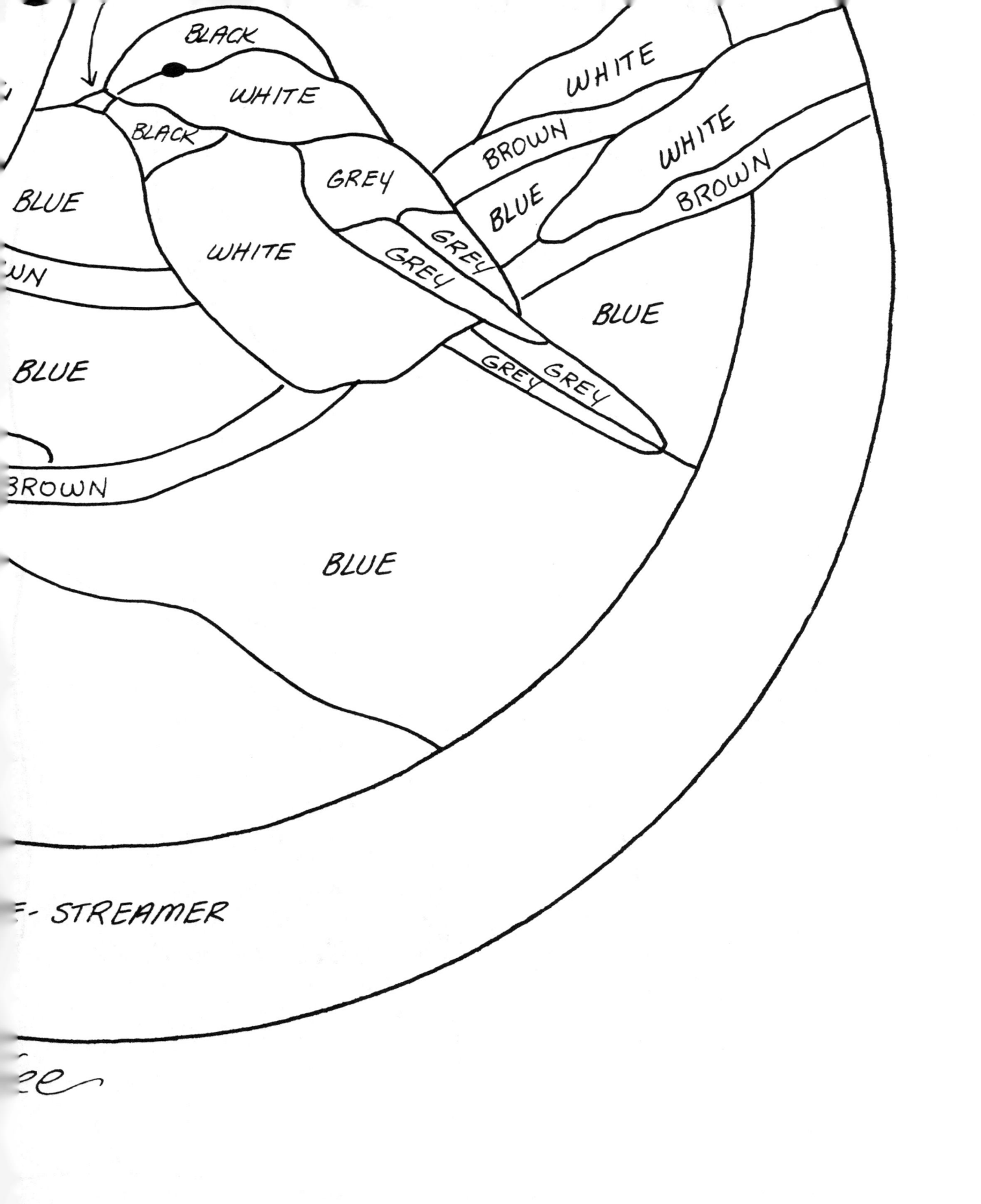

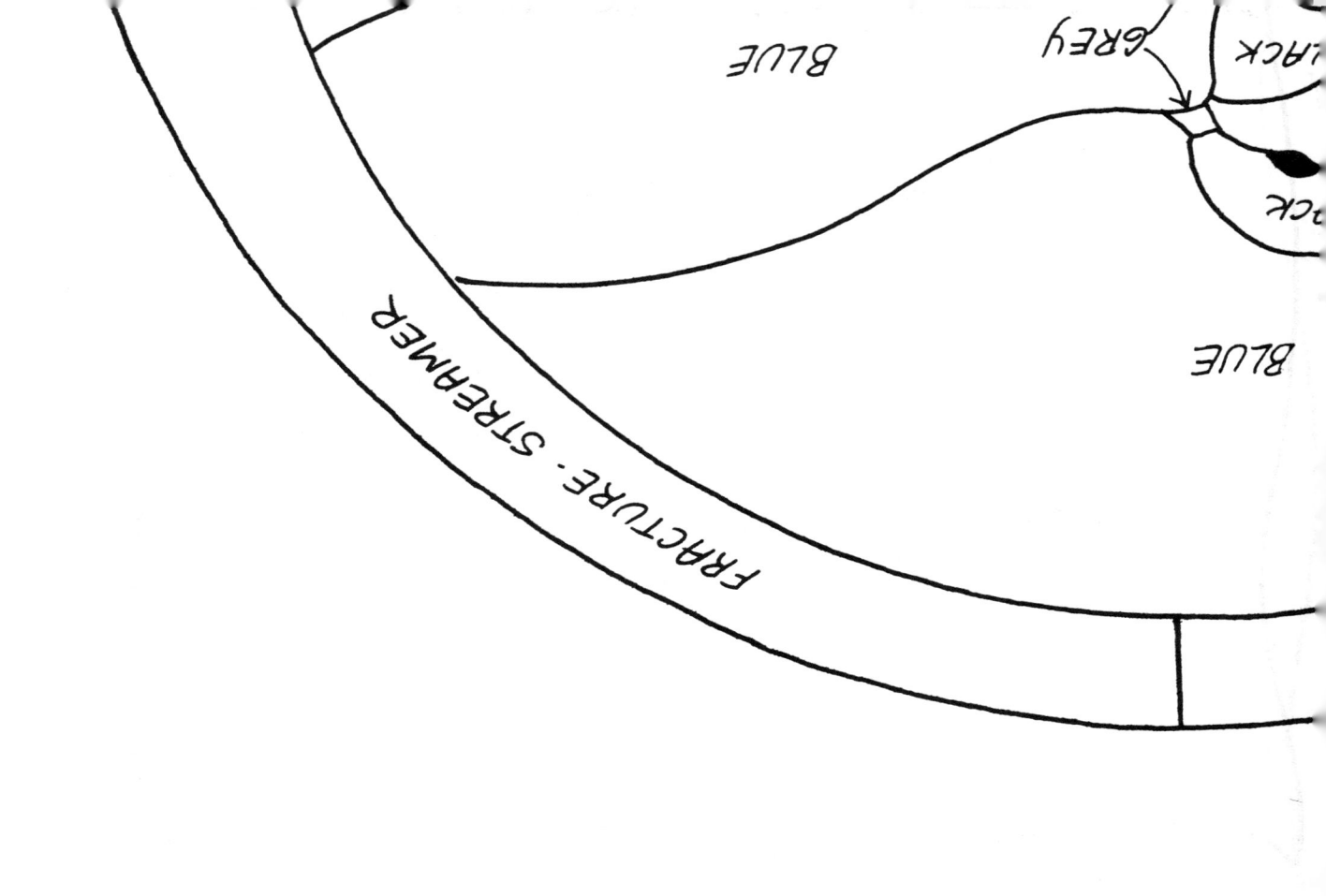

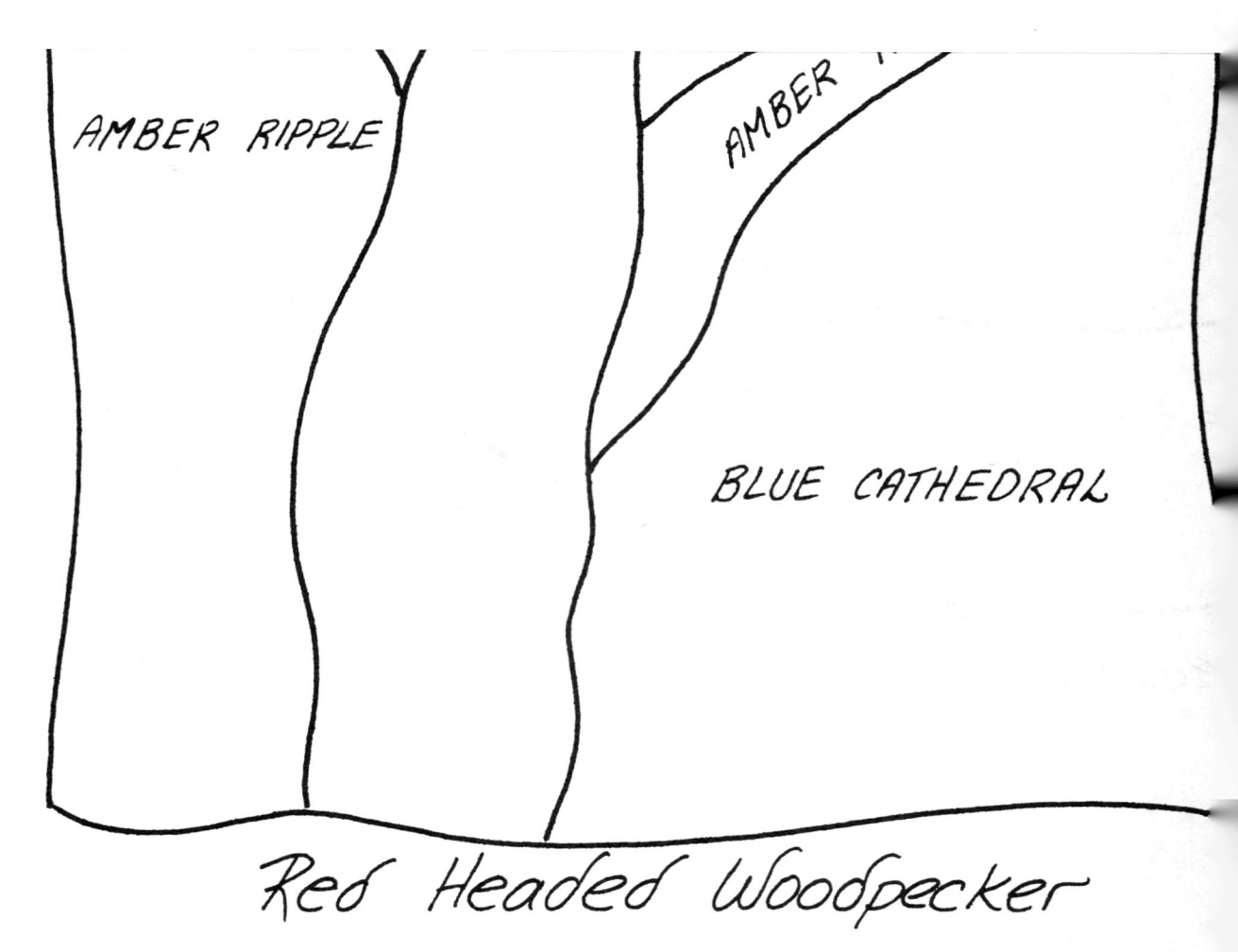

BLUE

GREY

BLACK

BLUE

BLUE

FRACTURE-STREAMER

AMBER RIPPLE

AMBER

BLUE CATHEDRAL

Red Headed Woodpecker

OPAL OPAL OPAL
CATHEDRAL OPAL CATHEDRAL

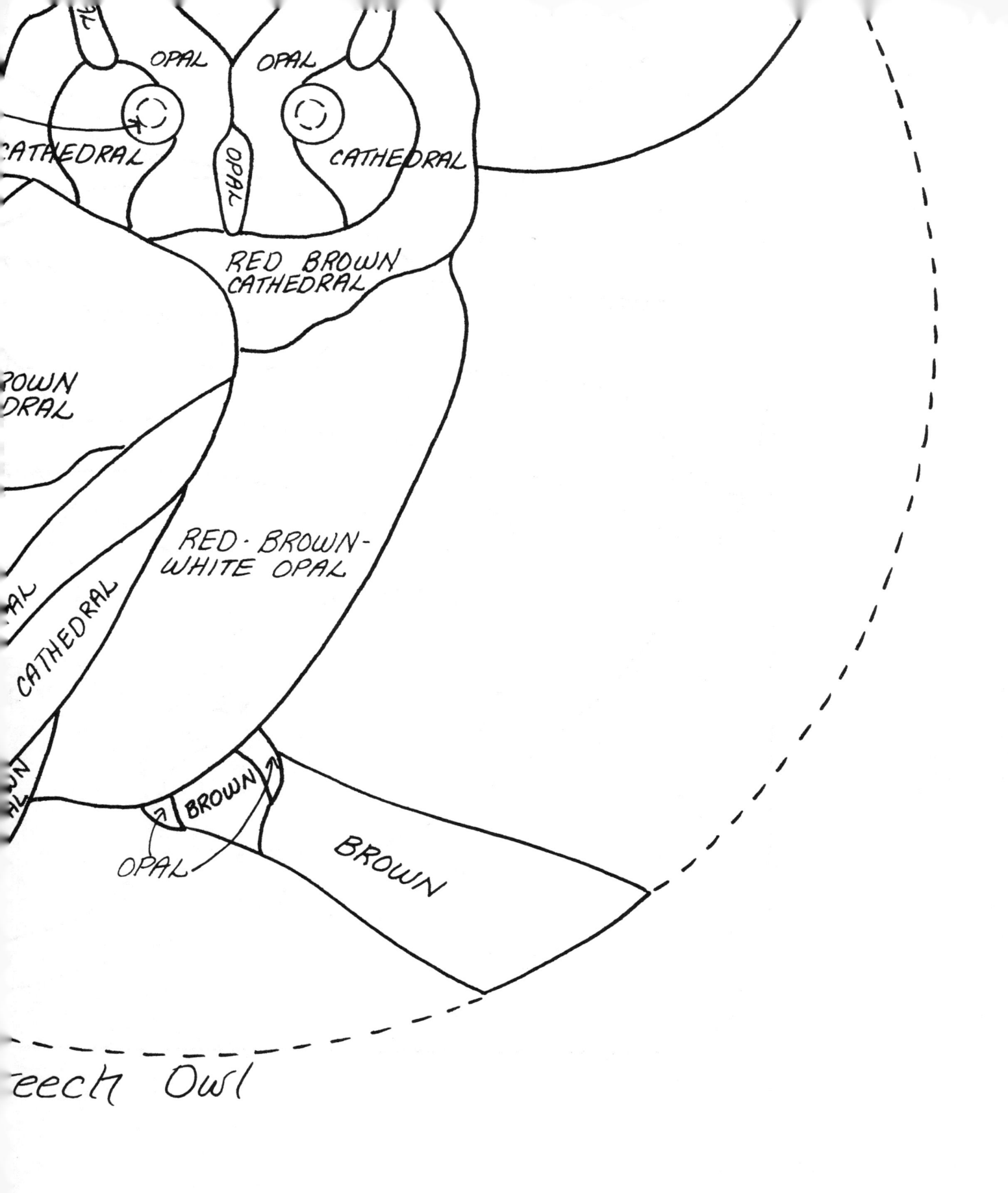

RED BROWN
CATHEDRAL

ROWN
DRAL

RED·BROWN-
WHITE OPAL

CATHEDRAL

BROWN

OPAL

BROWN

reech Owl

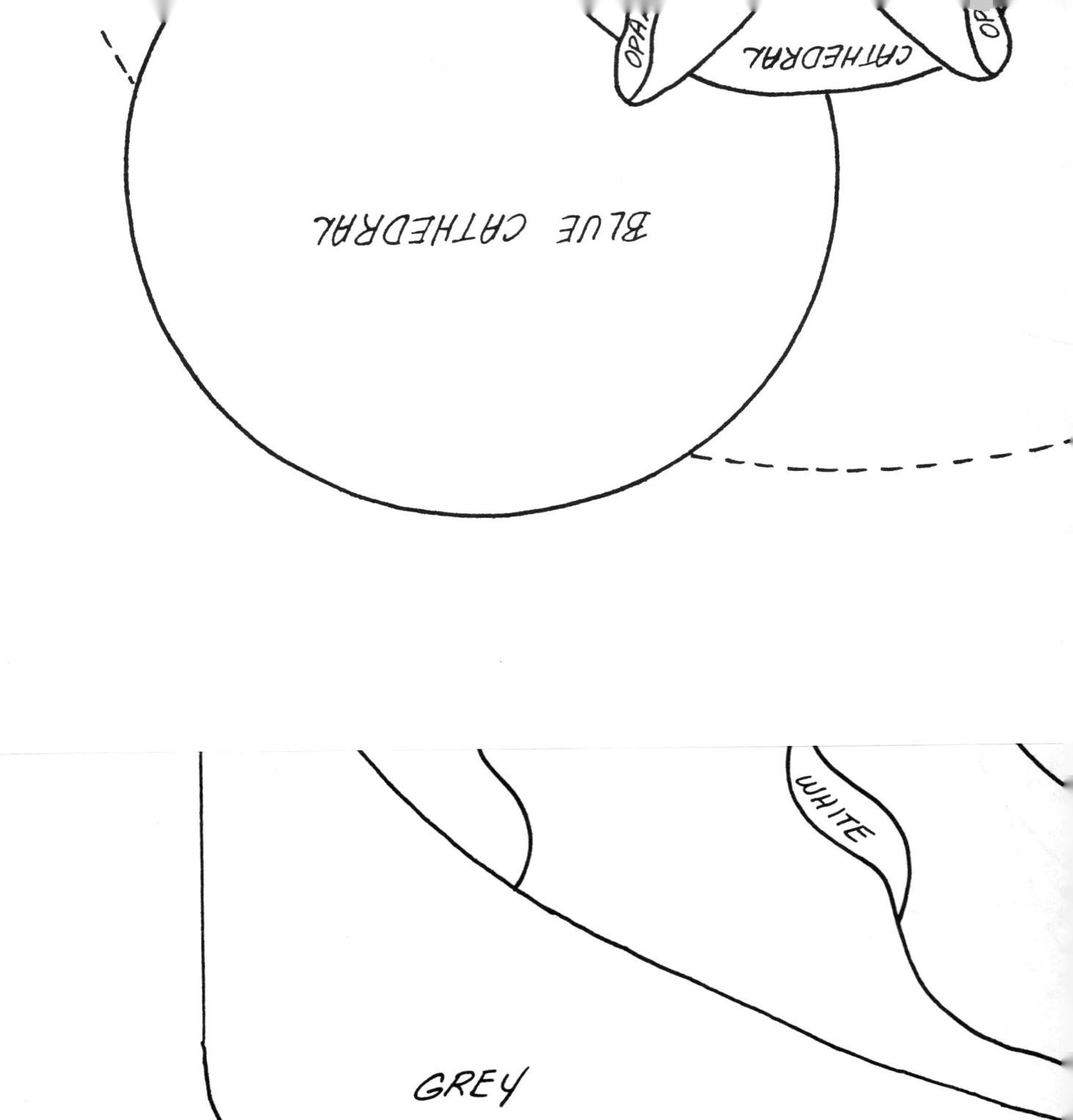

BLUE CATHEDRAL

OPAL
CATHEDRAL

WHITE

GREY

CATHEDRAL

LOOK

BLACK + CLEAR

BLACK +

WHITE

BLACK + CLEAR

WHITE

BLACK

BLACK

WHITE

BLACK

RED

BLACK

LT GREY

GOLD

BLACK

USE WIRE

GOLD

BLACK

GOLD

BLACK

GOLD

BLACK

## Harlequin Duck

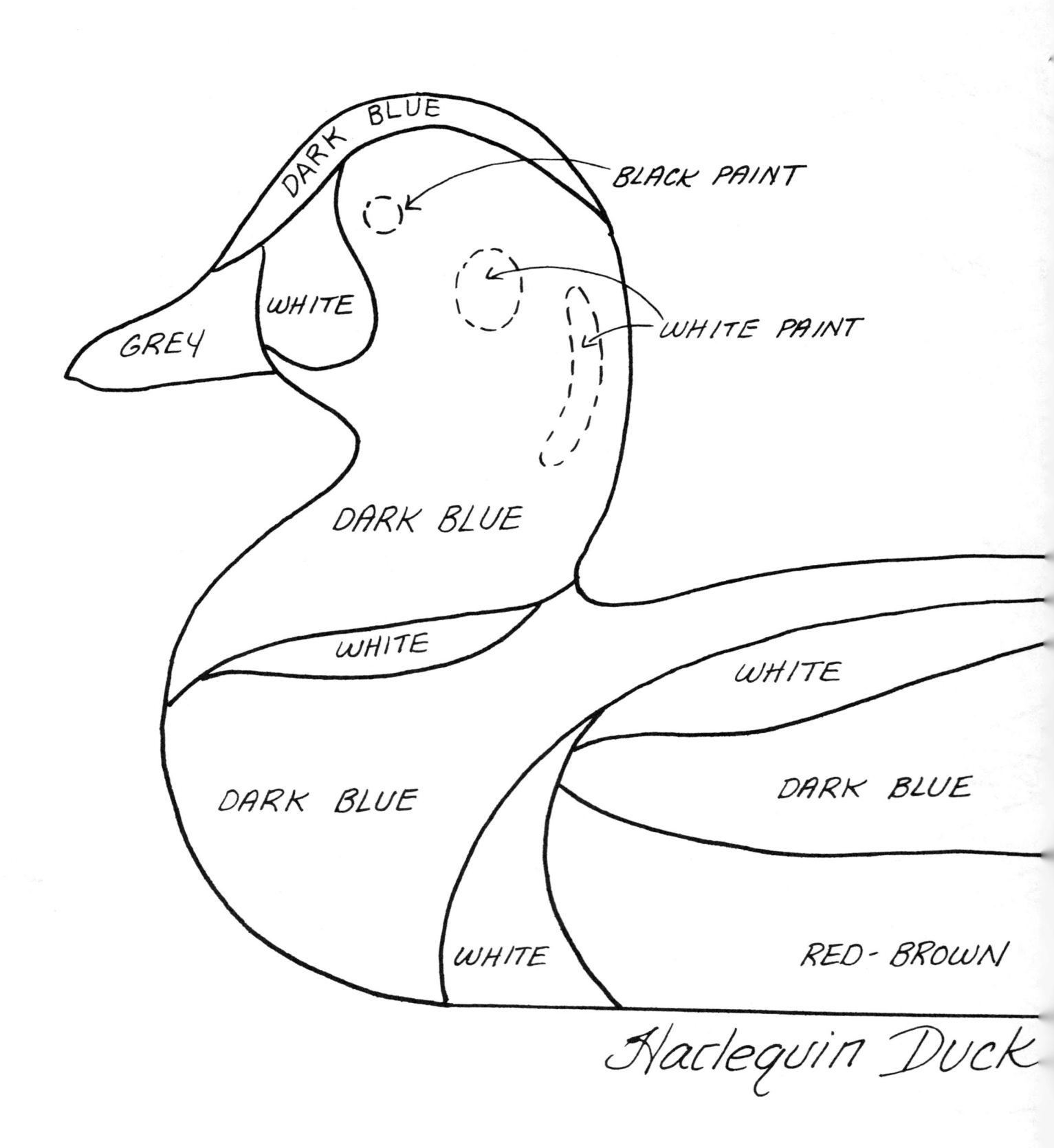

- DARK BLUE (head crown)
- BLACK PAINT (eye)
- WHITE (cheek patch)
- GREY (bill)
- WHITE PAINT (ear spot and neck stripe)
- DARK BLUE (neck/face)
- WHITE (neck ring)
- WHITE (shoulder stripe)
- DARK BLUE (breast)
- WHITE (flank stripe)
- DARK BLUE (wing)
- RED-BROWN (side)

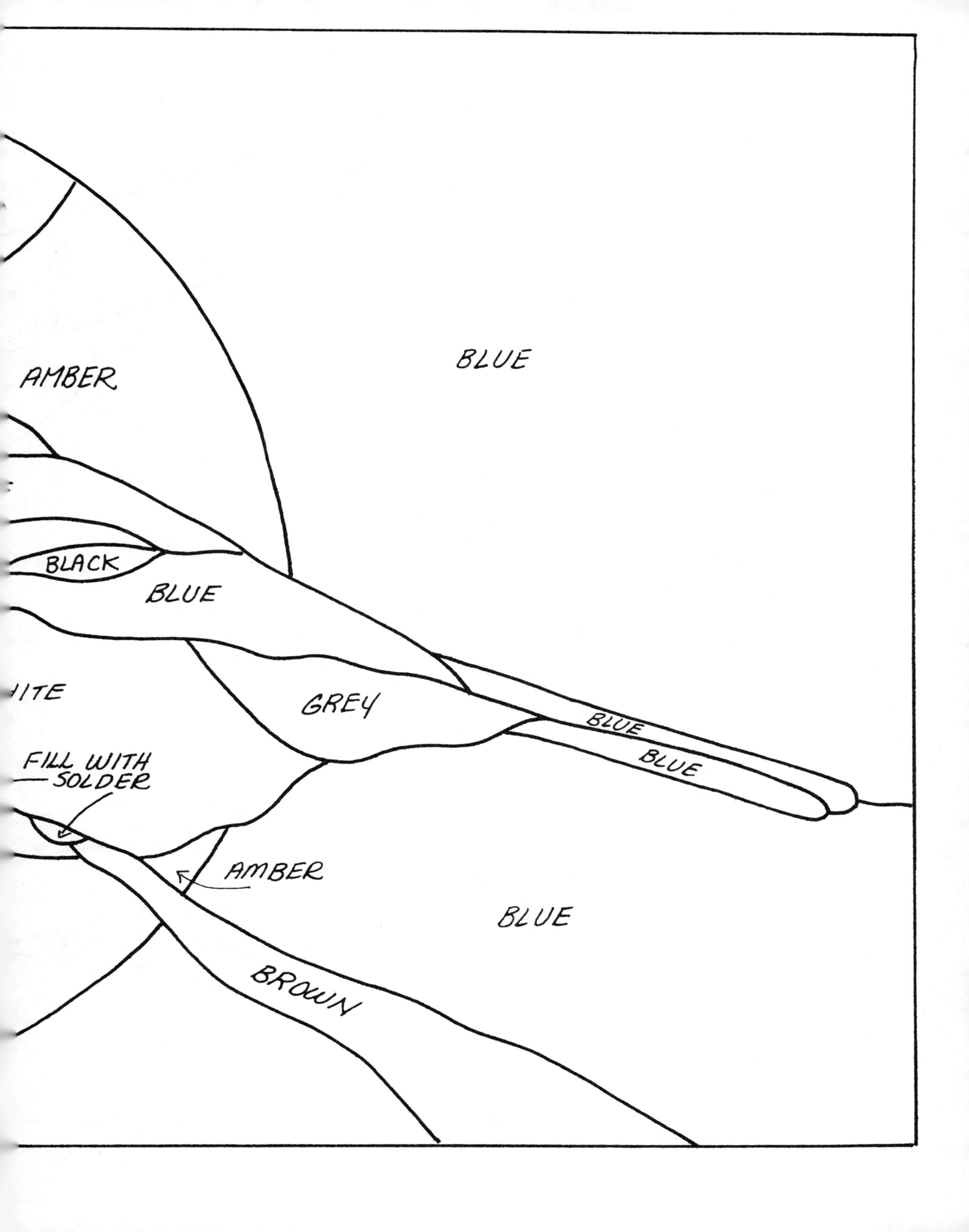

AMBER

BLUE

BLACK

BLUE

HITE

GREY

BLUE

BLUE

FILL WITH
SOLDER

AMBER

BLUE

BROWN

WIRE

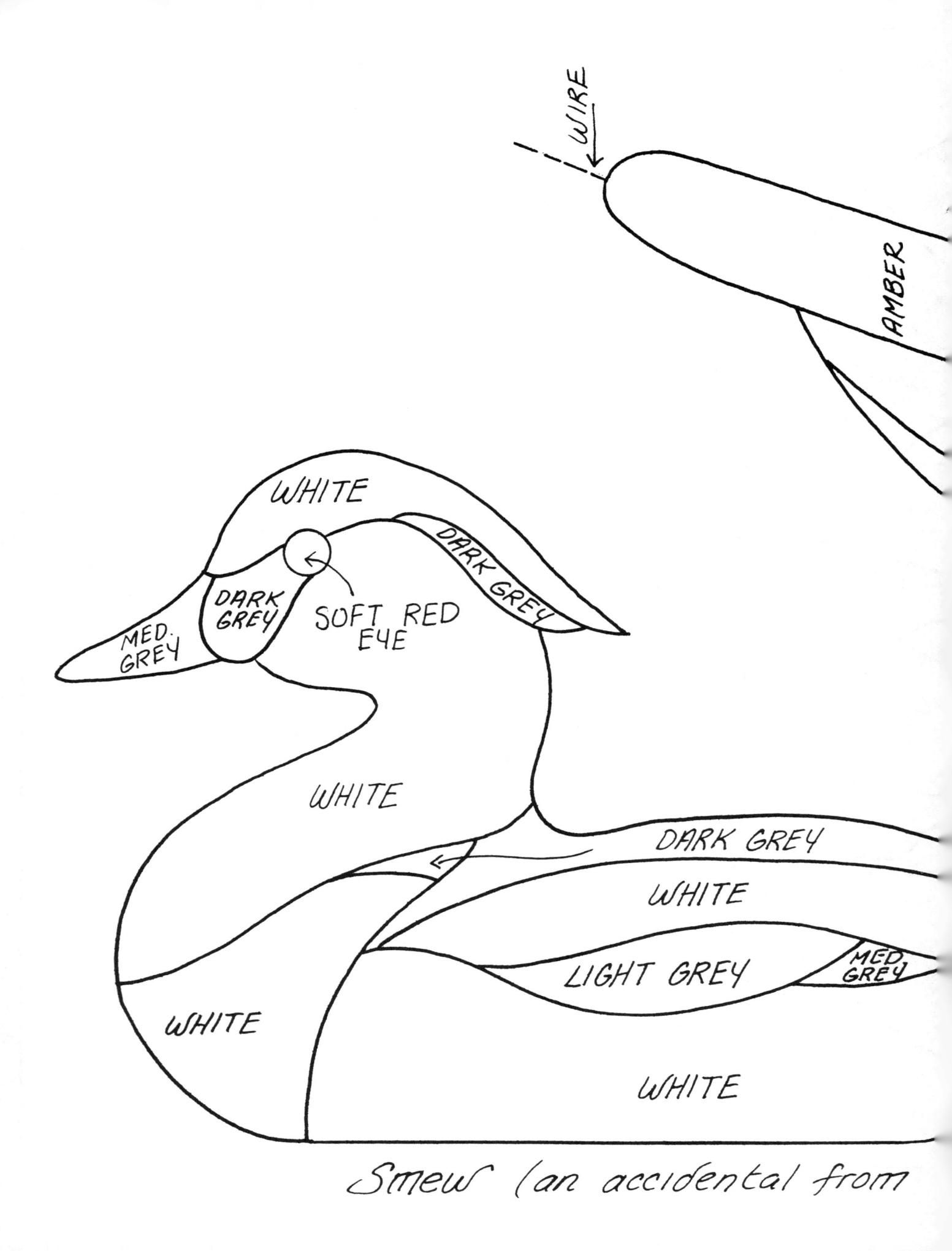

AMBER

WHITE

DARK GREY

MED. GREY

DARK GREY

SOFT RED EYE

WHITE

DARK GREY

WHITE

LIGHT GREY

MED GREY

WHITE

WHITE

Smew (an accidental from

# SPECIFICATIONS
# BIRD PANELS

## *Chickadee*

Dimensions: 13 inch circle

### MATERIALS

**Glass border** - White Fractures with black Streamers - 1 sq. ft.
**Sky** - Medium blue Antique or Cathedral - 1 sq. ft.
**Tree** - Green Opal - 1/2 sq. ft.
**Tree branch** - Brown - 1/3 sq. ft.
**Snow (on branch)** - White - 1/3 sq. ft.
**Chickadee** - Black, grey and white Opals
One length 1/4 inch U zinc or U lead for border

## *Hummingbird*

Dimensions: 12 inch circle

### MATERIALS

**Hummingbird** - Olive green Cathedral or Opal and red Cathedral
**Flower** - Bevel cluster JF 01-C or colored glass of your choice
**Leaves** - Bevel cluster JL-02 or green glass
**Background** - Amber Craquelle or Cathedral
**Glass Border** - Violet Cathedral
One length 1/4 inch U zinc or U lead for border

## *Red-Headed Woodpecker*

Dimensions: 7 inches wide by 15 inches high

### MATERIALS

**Woodpecker** - Red Cathedral for head, black, white and grey Opal
**Tree** - Dark brown Cathedral for hole, amber Ripple for trunk - 2/3 sq. ft.
**Sky** - Blue Cathedral - 2/3 sq. ft.
**Border** - 50 inches of ball chain or regular chain

### HINTS

It is important to solder either wire, chain or ball chain around the edge on top of the copper foil for sufficient support. See Glass Class Hints for further information.

# SPECIFICATIONS
# DUCK DECOYS

## Loon

**GLASS LIST**

Black
Black and Clear
White
Red (Eye)
Light Grey (Beak)

## Pintail

**GLASS LIST**

Dark Brown
Grey - light, medium, Opal and Cathedral
Gold
Black
White

## Smew
*(an accidental from Eurasia)*

**GLASS LIST**

White
Grey - light, medium and dark
Soft Red (Eye)

## Mallard

**GLASS LIST**

Green Irridescent
Yellow Opal (beak)
White
Brown - dark and light
Black
Grey - dark and light
Blue

# SPECIFICATIONS
# DUCK DECOYS

## Harlequin Duck

**GLASS LIST**
Dark Blue
White
Honey
Black
Grey

## Surf Scoter

**GLASS LIST**
Black
White
White with Orange patch

## Red-Breasted Merganser

**GLASS LIST**
Red Brown
Green
White Black Wispy
Black
Grey - dark and light

## American Wigeon

**GLASS LIST**
Green
Grey - light, medium and dark
White
Blue/Green (Beak)

# SPECIFICATIONS
# BIRD MOBILES

## *Goldfinch*

**GLASS LIST**
- Yellow
- Black
- White
- Brown
- Green

## *Cardinal*

**GLASS LIST**
- Red Cathedral
- Red Wispy
- Green
- Black
- Brown
- Orange (Beak)
- Grey (Eye)

14 gauge wire for legs and vine

## *Red-Winged Blackbird*

**GLASS LIST**
- Black
- Red
- Yellow
- Green
- Amber
- Brown
- Clear
- Grey (Beak)

Sheet foil for legs

# Walrus Publications
## presents

### ELEGANT LAMPS SERIES

Each book contains 16 new fullsize patterns for lampshades, many of which feature straight line bevels. The projects vary in difficulty to satisfy both the beginning and professional craftsperson. Basic lamp construction techniques are outlined in the Glass Class section and many tricks of the trade are offered throughout this book. Each pattern is supplied with all the information you need to construct the project.

### BIRDS OF NORTH AMERICA
#### Vol. 1 & 2

These books will help to bring the beauty of nature into your home. Included are 17 fullsize patterns for small panels and mobiles of a variety of birds plus decoy-style duck designs. There is a project here for everyone from beginner to experienced craftsperson. If you love birds you will love this book.

### DISTINCTIVE VASES

The projects in this book were developed over a period of a few years from a desire to create objects out of stained glass which could be displayed on tables, buffets, fireplace mantles, etc.; and that would look good in ambient light. Dried flowers will enhance some designs, but most of them look great on their own.

**Walrus Publications**

587 Sargent Ave., Winnipeg, MB Canada    R3B 1W6    Telephone: (204) 783-1117